THE MEMORY BOX

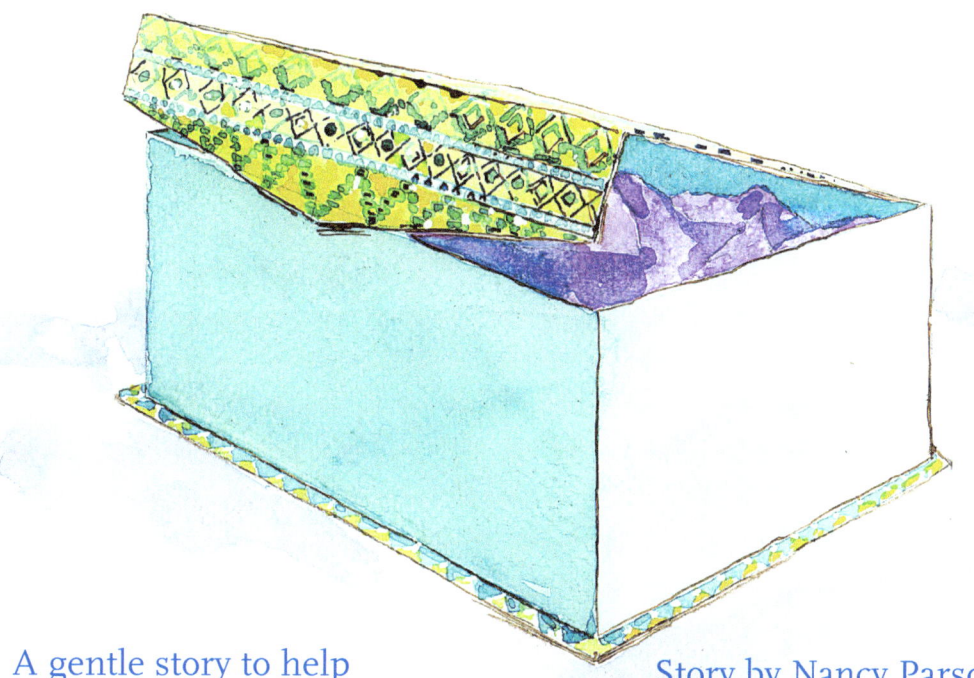

A gentle story to help challenged adults understand death

Story by Nancy Parsons
Illustrations by Don Doyle

THE MEMORY BOX
Nancy Parsons

Published by The Cheshire Press
an imprint of The Cheshire Group
Andover, MA 01810
www.cheshirepress.com

All rights reserved. No part of this book may be reproduced or transmitted in any form or by any means without the express written consent of the author, except for the inclusion of quotations in reviews.

Copyright (c) 2018 by Linda Burke

ISBN: 978-0-9995092-5-8

Library of Congress Control Number: 218938151

Printed in the United States of America

All trademarks used herein are for identification only and are used without intent ro infringe on the owner's trademarks or other property rights

Illustrations by Don Doyle

Dedicated to the gentle memory of
David Burke

You are so loved

My name is Lisa. I'm going to tell you a story. It's a sad story but it's a happy story too. It's a story about my dad and his memory box.

My dad's name was David and he always said he loved me. I know a lot about some things and there are things I don't know much about. But I do know this—I know my dad loved me.

And I know he still does.

But my dad got sick. Very sick. And after a time, we knew he couldn't get well. Reverend Rick told me that my dad would be going to Heaven to live in God's house. He said it wouldn't be easy for Dad to leave me and our family. But Reverend Rick knew it would be hard for us too, so he asked me to think about something.

"Think how beautiful Heaven is," he said. "I want you to think about the house where your dad will live. And I'd like you to think about the people who are waiting for him in that house."

So I thought about that.

"Will Bumpa be there?" I asked. Bumpa is my grandfather and he has been in Heaven for a long time.

"Most certainly," Reverend Rick said. "He is waiting for your dad right now. And when the time is right, Bumpa will come and take your dad to Heaven. You won't see him come, but he'll be there. Your dad will see him though. Think how happy they will be to be together again."

That made me happy, thinking about Dad and Bumpa together in Heaven, but it made me unhappy to think how I would feel to be left behind.

"What can I do with my sad feelings?" I asked.

"I think it's time to make memory boxes," my sister Kris said.

I had never heard of a memory box and maybe you haven't either. So let me tell you about a memory box.

It is a box that holds the most special memories of good times. It holds the memories you most want to keep, so you have to think very hard and choose only the best and happiest of memories to put in the box.

"Dad will have a memory box," Kris said. "It will be very big, of course, because it will have to hold lots of memories. A lot of people will have memories of Dad that they will want to put in it."

My memory box—the box for my memories of Dad—was just regular size. But it was also very special because the memories in it would be those shared just between the two of us.

This is my memory box.

And this is what's in it.

I put in an airplane—just a toy one—to remind Dad of the trips we took to DisneyWorld. Seven trips! Seven! And each trip was packed with fun.

I put in pictures we took at Disney of my family having Disney-fun. Mom, Dad, Kris, and Dina. And me, of course. We all had big smiles because it was such a happy time.

I put in some purple stones. Purple is my favorite color. I think everyone loves purple because it is such a happy color. You don't find purple stones every day, but when you do find one, you know it is a special day. Dad gave me a purple stone shaped like a heart. It is one of my most favorite things.

I put in a block of wood that says: I love that you're my DAD. I thought that was a nice memory for Dad to keep.

I put in my book of *Charlotte's Web*. It is the story of a baby pig whose life is saved by a little girl who loves him very much. Dad read that book to me again and again and I think he loved it as much as I do. I think it is my favorite book of all time.

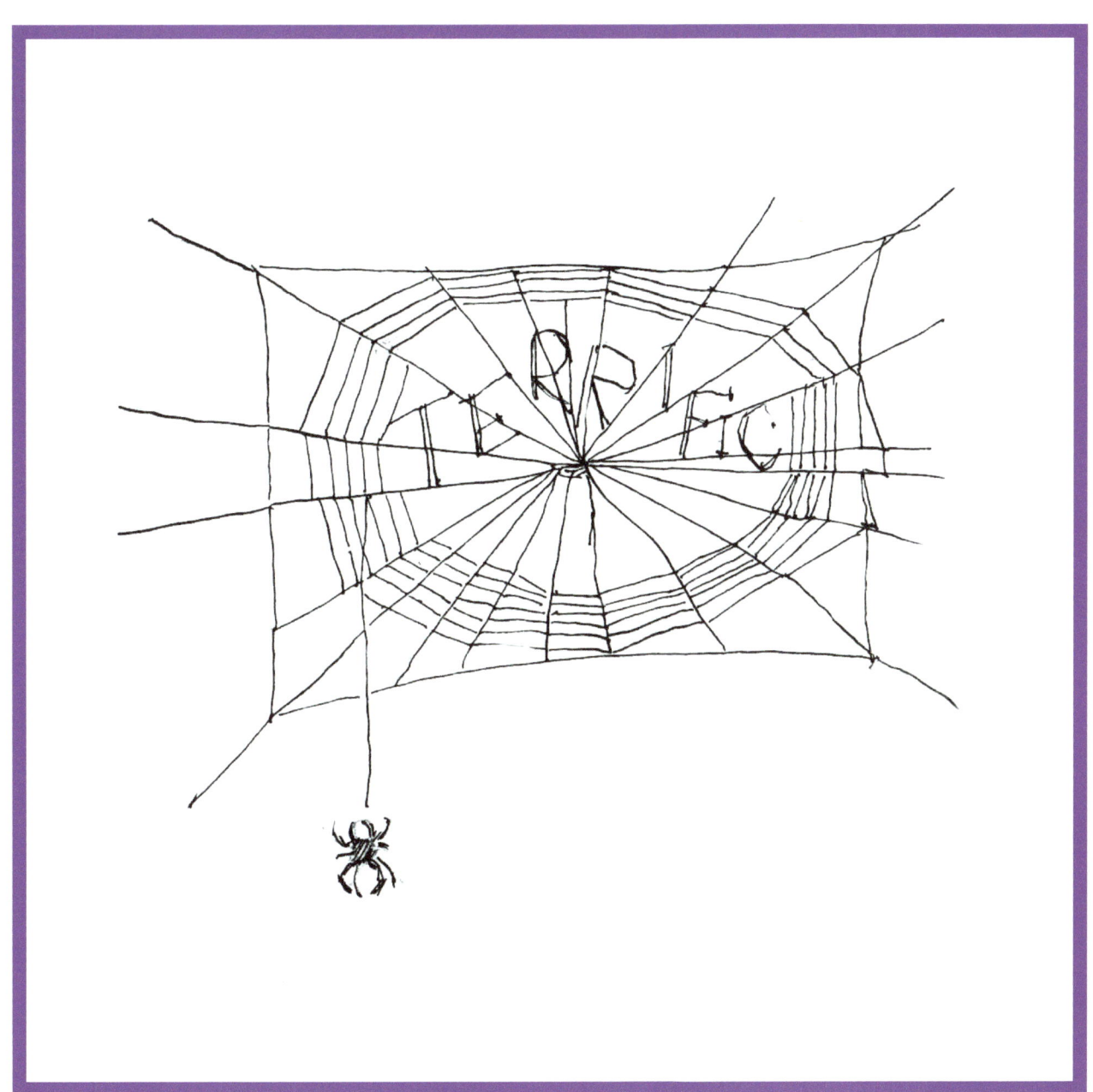

When the time came for Bumpa to silently come and take Dad's hand and lead him to Heaven, Dad was very happy. He and Bumpa always laughed together a lot. It's nice that they are together again. Bumpa will take Dad's memory box to Heaven too but no one will see him come, and no one, but Dad, will hear him.

"Will God take care of Dad?" I asked Mom.

"Yes, Lisa," she said. "God will most certainly take care of your dad."

We had a church service to say good-by to my dad. Let me tell you why this is important. People need a place to say good-by, and they needed a time to share their memories of my dad.

Just as Kris had said, Dad's memory box was very big because it had to hold all the memories people brought. Our whole family came— Mom and my sisters and brothers-in-law. My nephews and nieces. All the aunts and uncles and friends and neighbors were there. Reverend Rick was there too. He and I walked to Dad's memory box carrying my smaller memory box. We placed my little box on top of Dad's big one, right next to the flowers that were from me.

"Everyone in church will see your memory box on top of your dad's," Reverend Rick said. "You'll be sitting in the front of the church so you will be able to see everything."

The church was filled with people. I knew they were all thinking about Dad and remembering things about him. He was a good joke teller. He was a good laugher too. And he was kind. That's what they were remembering, I know that for sure.

There was music and it made me happy, especially when we sang "On Eagle's Wings". That was my dad's favorite song. We sang it together every time I came in the house. Michael Crawford sang it with us, and Dad said he sounded nearly as good as we did. That song makes me so happy. I peeked at Mom and she was smiling too.

I looked one last time at the memory boxes in front of the church—the big, beautifully polished one that was Dad's and the little one that held the purple heart-shaped stone and *Charlotte's Web*. They made me feel happy.

Whenver my dad and I left each other, he always said the same thing: "Always remember I love you, Lisa," he'd say. "Forever and always. Now I want to see your beautiful smile."

So I am smiling now. Smiling just for him.

So this is my story. And it is my dad's story. But sooner or later, it is everybody's story. And this is what I want to tell you. This is what I want you to understand. We have our memories forever—forever and always.

www.ingramcontent.com/pod-product-compliance
Lightning Source LLC
Chambersburg PA
CBHW040057160426
43192CB00002B/96